a human story

living beyond the box

Carol Dumsday

ISBN 978-0-620-77869-5
Self-published
www.wellness-counselling.co.za

Cover design - Paddy Burke Design & Illustration
Printed and bound by Pixo-Print on Demand, Western Cape.

Authors note

My psychology counselling degree is the backdrop of my practice. Wellness Counselling was set up in 2010 as a space for my intention: to support and counsel people on a soul level, interfacing and balancing with human life in the present time.

Healing starts with Awareness, which is the important switch from our external to our internal power.

Our human experience shifts as we embrace our gift of free will and creativity. Through acknowledging our pain body, we explore new thought pathways to transform our life into healing and living well.

Contents

Introduction

As are you, I am a visitor here. I am defined by my humanness during my stay. But I suspect I'm much more than that, a part of a much bigger picture — perhaps a significant speck of all things connected?

I have been given my name: Carol, and I acknowledge the journey I have signed up for. My life, although unique, is full of the same hardships and challenges, tears and joy, frustration and beauty as yours.

So why this book? Life here is hard. And through the trickles and streams from wise and guiding souls we are awakening to the truth of our being: that we are creative souls and with this gift, we have free will to design our life's intention.

Through this book, I hope to start a conversation about our choices to live life on Earth in wellness in the present time.

We all have unique stories and experiences. When we are able to acknowledge our story as separate from our being, we have a clearer view to observe the gifts that our stories bring in the form of life's upheavals. For me, one of my defining moments was shown after a prolonged trauma in my personal life. Through this experience my world was 'properly' turned upside down. I received a huge 'shake-up' from the universe. It was only once the trauma had passed that I was able to look back and see that this opportunity had allowed me to make some positive changes in both my work and my relationships. And through this experience, I was 'nudged' to follow my passion and to pursue my psychology studies.

There were some detours along the way as I found myself juggling studies, being a full-time working mom and there were times when the load was really heavy and I put my plans on hold. As it is with life, when our passion is aligned with our intent, opportunities showed themselves. And I was fortunate that I was able to pick up my course work again and to graduate with a psychology counselling degree. I had a calling and desire to work with people in a healing environment — but I had no idea how wonderful and rewarding this work would really be.

Along the way we all receive signposts from the universe, mostly ignored — flicked away like the high pitch frequency of a mosquito flying close to our ear. When we ignore those nudges the shake-up happens to get our attention. Sound familiar?

Through my work and passion the universe has issued the aforementioned 'nudge' to share this message of free will and creativity as the core of our humanness. Sharing this message attempts to guide and support us in finding our path to awareness and living well. As we are all inter-connected, this message forms a part of soul consciousness, of which I am just one of the tellers.

Through experiences and reflections, I have come to realise that both our humanness and our environment create our desired experiences which enable us to evolve. In this expansion, we have our part to play as potential contributors to the soul consciousness.

We are all struggling. I hope this book, in its simplicity, offers some insights and encourages us on our path. Its intention is to support us as we navigate our path to a more comfortable, passionate and truthful life.

A human story introduces the 'life-box' which is the life that we create for ourselves, on a conscious and unconscious level. When we are mindful and aware, we create and extend our life-box in our own truth.

There is a lot of noise in our environment. It is a world of immediate information overload. When we quiet our mind, we uplift our soul to connect with the divine. The answers we receive through our inner vibrations and the whisperings of the soul are the all-knowing truth. Possibly we have chosen the events we need to encounter and the lessons we wish to learn? But the important bit is how we respond to our experiences from our unique environment and in our interactions with others. Our response determines how we live. We can choose to live in stress or in wellness, as we negotiate the seasons and storms of our life as they present themselves.

We are here for a relatively short time, yet we have many paths to travel, and not every path we encounter will be comfortable. But when we are aware we can make decisions that will enhance our well-being and the quality of our life-box. With awareness we are better equipped to take courageous steps to healing, to start the process of re-modelling our life-box with its foundations in wellness. Healing allows us to find our way back to who we are, to release our story, stand in our power and let go of that which no longer serves us. We acknowledge that our story is just that: one of our stories. It is not who we are, but it is our human being having an experience. It does not define us.

As we explore and journey, it is important to remember to add sparkle and fun to our life-box. After all, we can't take our time here too seriously, it is a flash in time and we can live well, as our true self is always safe.

We are all unique; each of us will experience the world differently. What we do share is the need to find a balance between our human being living comfortably with our environment and our soul's purpose.

Two

The Journey to now

"We are spiritual beings
having a human experience"

We are all a little lost. We are searching. Perhaps the search is, the way back to our true nature.

This is a human story ...

I am seven years old. I am not comfortable in the world. A childhood spent unknowingly meditating; daydreaming, sitting in trees, floating in water, in pools and the ocean. Perhaps awake and connected to spirit, but not fully present in the world. My younger self wasn't very accomplished at fitting in.

My mother, a pragmatic parent, thought that I was a square peg in a round hole — and recognised that I was not comfortable here in the world. She supported me in the hope of making life easier by guiding me to follow the rules and fit in. As I didn't adjust well to institutional and social norms, my younger self either questioned authority or just went about my life in a way that made sense to me. This found me in trouble with authority figures and I was sometimes labelled 'rebel'? My intention, however, was trying to make sense of the world. I felt disconnected from this world. It was like some pieces of the puzzle were missing. But as the years passed by I observed life around me and worked out how to fit in and started to lay down foundations for my life-box.

Our arrival in this world begins with awareness, we are not born with concepts and ideas of how the world operates. And so it is that sometime from our birth we begin to observe, absorb and interact with the world around us and start subconsciously constructing our life-box. Its foundations seeped in the values and belief systems of our families, communities and countries. Our life-box is the space we create where we establish our human identity based on the feedback from our environment. Through the verbal and non-verbal communication we receive from our environment is how we form our perceptions and ideas. These become the windows of our life-box.

My path too began with awareness and through the societal systems I lost my sense of awareness. After a time I began to build my life-box to the speculations and directions of others, proving to be a very uncomfortable experience but I started to fit in and received some approving nods. My current self is finding the way back to awareness. I am thankful that, through my experiences and nudges from the universe, I am extending and exploring beyond the confines of my life-box.

Through our unique circumstances, we start on our path to awareness. Incidentally, it was a book that found me at exactly the right time that resonated deeply with me. It was like the pieces of a puzzle starting to fall into place. This book "Through love into healing" is written by the author Dr. Brian Weiss in which he spoke of the permanence of the soul. He has an impressive list of qualifications in both the medical and scientific field and is a qualified medical doctor who specialised in psychiatry. This book records some case studies and events that took place during his counselling sessions with patients, when using hypnosis. The hypnosis technique is sometimes used for patients who need to go deeper into the subconscious to unblock the challenges and hardships that they experience in their lives. During some of these hypnosis sessions he stumbled upon past lives. Initially he dismissed these encounters as imagination and vivid dreams, until there came a time when he found that he could no longer ignore the information that was being channeled through his patients. He had to question his careful constructions of how he understood the world. With his notable academic history, by default Dr Weiss is an authority figure.

We tend to unconsciously kick into sheep mode and accept an authority's words as absolute truth. However, trust your truth — that which resonates with you and question that which does not, taking care not to fall into the 'authority trap'.

We should be mindful when receiving information and listen for the vibration deep down inside us. This is the way that we know if the information we are receiving resonates with us; when the question and answer are simultaneously answered. Our head and the heart are aligned. This is the language of our soul, our inner voice that guides us to our truth.

I continued to read literature on the permanence of the soul, with soul energy as our true nature. My human nature and conditioning finds equanimity that this belief is supported by scientists, fathers of psychology and religious leaders.

Having a natural passion for people and their stories, and starting on my personal path to awareness, coincided with the beginnings of my psychology studies. I had a strong desire to work with people in a counselling environment. Humanness, healing and soul were the words that resounded in my being. As I mentioned before — when our intent is aligned with our passion, opportunities present themselves. We have the choice to take a step forward, leading us to the next step on our life's path.

The more I live, the more human stories I hear and the more healing I witness at soul level through our humanness — the more humbled I am; as I acknowledge all that is.

Soul purpose unfolds through human experience and we should reflect on how we are experiencing our time here in our human being. Humanness is who we are in the world. It is temporary; it is a vehicle that we use to experience the world and to facilitate the necessary lessons that propel our soul growth to a higher consciousness. Soul is who we are, our true self. My work attempts to balance consciousness and awareness with our humanness in the present time.

The universe plays its part as it nudges us towards awareness, however ultimately it is our decision how we choose to live. We have free will and can choose to close our hearts during the difficult times we encounter or to open our hearts and embrace the path of our humanness and soul.

As we journey toward a more comfortable world, we should know that there is a difference between awareness and thought. Awareness is our spirit and thought is our ego. In other words, thought is the filter we put on an experience, awareness is the experience.

Our human being experiences the world uniquely and based on our perceptions, which are our thought filters, we view and experience our world. Our stories are unique. They are stories we build through our memories and experiences. And all our stories are important as they impact the conscious whole; so we should take utmost care to understand our stories. We need to know that, although our story is a part of us, we are not our story. We need to heal past hurts to find our way from helplessness to take back our power. As we start to heal, we acknowledge our story: letting it go as we bravely begin to live beyond our story.

We have little control over what life throws our way; we can only control how we respond to the situation. Our response impacts our journey and we should all have some useful tools in our life-box to positively manage that which life hurls at us.

Building high walls of brick and mortar closes our heart and keeps our life-box small. To heal we have to keep an open heart full of gratitude and love.

We can expand our life-box by letting go of fear and self-beliefs that hold us back from our potential. Let go of the masks we wear, the worldview and belief systems that no longer serve us.

Three

The Life-box

"There is a crack in everything,
that's how the light gets in" ~
Leonard Cohen

Our life-box is the space of perceived safety which our human being creates. It is from this perspective that we experience and view our world.

Our human identity starts at birth. And sometime after our arrival in the world we begin to construct our life-box, starting with our foundations that are grounded in the values, belief systems, rituals and traditions of our family and community.

It is together with our conscious and unconscious learnings and how we have been affected by our environment that will impact the filter we choose to put over our experiences. These perceptions are the windows of our life-box.

As the years pass by we encounter our life experiences and unconsciously we add various coping strategies to our life-box. We acquire defence mechanisms largely through our negative experiences, these defences 'help' us cope with our lives as they protect deep hurts. They are on high alert for perceived future threats and are ready to attack. Some of us are so defended, unknowingly we carry so much artillery that our life-box becomes our fort.

Not only does the life-box encompass our human identity, our soul consciousness is in the mix too. Our consciousness is the awareness of our existence, sensations and surroundings.

In our life-box we find our emotional, physical, mental and spiritual self. The facets of the self do not exist in isolation and are all inter-linked and interdependent. For example, when we get ill our body suffers from physiological symptoms, the causes are often linked to our emotional body. Our spiritual body is the peaceful awareness and expansion of prayer or meditation around our presenting illness. Our mental thinking is the 'thought filter' we use to determine how we will experience our illness.

The physical body is the appearance of our human being; our genetics and birthplace largely determine our gender, race and nationality. Our physical body includes our overall health and body functioning.

Our mental self is our mind constructs, and it conceptualises the world as we experience our environment. Here we acquire empirical knowledge and reasoning skills. We make decisions for our physical, emotional and spiritual being, ensuring that our life-box is safe. Our thinking is influenced by the thought filter we put over our experiences. The thought-filter we choose is the link to our emotional intelligence. When we have emotional intelligence we choose to use filters that will uplift others in our interactions, we choose to build healthy relationships rather than engaging in destructive communications.

Our emotional self encompasses our experiences that provoke feelings and is the link to our soul as it impacts our soul's growth. As we learn our emotional lessons we expand the consciousness of the soul.

Emotional lessons are the gifts wrapped up in the lessons we learn. These include taking responsibility for our actions and not blaming others; being tolerant of the beliefs and values of others and letting go of that which is not meant for us. There are many emotional lessons we may have chosen to learn. The all-important emotional lesson for humanity as encountered through our humanness is awareness; to be non-judgmental observers and empathetic to others which leads to compassion. Compassion leads to love and love is the language of the soul.

Our spiritual self is the connectedness of all that is. It is tolerant and accepting of all humanity, and it is awareness of an experience without a thought filter.

We are born with knowing, a sense of something we can't quite remember; it is vague and just out of our reach, like a glimpse in 'the corner of our senses' of something that we can't quite grab a hold of. This is the awareness of the soul. As our brain engages we kick into thinking and out of 'being.' We then lose this feeling of something we are not quite remembering.

Our body and mind encompass our humanness; as we know our human life here is temporary. We receive constant reminders from the environment of our mortality and how quickly a life passes by. We should all be encouraged to take down the brick walls, expand our life-box, by exploring, journeying and living well. Our true self is permanent, it cannot be harmed or destroyed, be burnt or get wet. It is always safe.

Our greatest human traits are our ability to adapt and to survive in our environment. As we live in the now, we want to be as comfortable as possible. How do we do this? Have we understood the real meaning of safety and comfort? Is it allowing external chaos and fear to drive us into our fort-box with high walls, security, and artillery? Or do we take steps to becoming aware by taking down the brick walls of our life-box? This will allow us to live in a more permeable environment with our well-being emanating from our internal voice, thus restoring our 'being' which in turn positively impacts ourselves and humanity.

When we are unconsciously surviving in our life-box and learning by osmosis, we become a sheep-like community blindly following the crowd and checking in to see we are doing the 'right' thing. Societies and communities require laws or there would be chaos in our world. However, we need to step out of our life-box comfort zone to embrace our personal freedom; that is the freedom of thought, the freedom to be curious, to be courageous and to question that which does not sit well with our inner self.

I am heartened at the wave of consciousness. Our human beings are starting to question the norms, to explore new ideas, to question establishment and to look at new opportunities. This is humanity bravely taking back its power.

It is the brave who have trusted their beliefs, followed their passions and become the pioneers in their fields. There was a time when humankind thought the world was flat. One man took on mankind and despite the ridicule he persisted; to prove that the earth is in fact round. Brave women took great risks so that future women could vote and have equal opportunity in the workplace. One man went to prison for 27 years to ensure freedom for his country.

We do not have to be political leaders, feminist activists or scientists to take steps outside the box. We make these changes so that we become pioneers of our own life-box. The small steps we take really do expand our lives and touch all that is good in the name of humankind. Critical mass, which is the sufficient input from humanity to have a significant impact will expand communities, and then humanity is able to evolve as a conscious whole toward a new and more peaceful existence.

We are the designers and the directors of our lives. We have free will to choose how we create our life-box. We decide on its size, how it looks, how it interacts with the world and whether the walls are permeable or are prison walls. Through our unique interactions, we choose our 'thought filters' we use over our experiences.

Through our life-box, we encounter our environment, our relationships, and our work. As we continuously interact with our circumstances on planet Earth at the present time, the all-important question is "how are we experiencing our environment, our relationships and, our work life?"

There is an underlying human self-sabotaging factor that holds huge sway on the build of our life-box: this is a lack of self-belief — a human condition. Self-belief underlies all that we aspire to be and depending on how we embrace the self, will measure what we are able to achieve during our time here. To believe in ourselves and our abilities is key to stepping forward into the fullness of our passions.

Four

How we experience and react to the world

"Out beyond the ideas of right and wrong there is a field, I will meet you there" ~ Rumi

Through our unique view from our life-box, we encounter the world.

The world is not always a nice place. We negotiate some treacherous terrain. Sometimes people are horrible — they are unaware and their ignorance and anger disguise deeply buried pain as they readily engage in negativity at any opportunity.

As pain unconsciously wields its defences it can be metamorphosed into inflated ego, fear-driven, and often misused power. This pain manifests itself through abusive human interaction, often using platforms such as propaganda and social media to hold other humans in fear. And so it is that these hurt humans may also choose to inflict their pain on others through their relationships or using the cloak of social media. Bullying and nasty comments are a mirror for human pain and are not a reflection of the intended receiver. By hurting others, it unconsciously hopes to lessen the burden of the pain body who does not yet know there is a path to healing. When we are aware we can consciously choose who and what to engage with. We choose to direct our senses, tune our eyes and ears toward that which guides us on our path to wellness.

Try not to be drawn into that which is negative in our environment, social media and on the internet. We have free will to make these choices for our life-box. I read that Elizabeth Gilbert an author and inspirational writer, never Googles herself. This is very sound advice as the naysayers are ready to attack by bullying or criticising others for their beliefs, life choices or anything for that matter.

We don't like criticism. If we are unaware we immerse ourselves in the external negative energies and it stops us from being courageous; to walk in our power and to live our truth. When we connect with our inner self we allow a passage for our authentic voice. When we recognise and embrace other humans whose intent it is to have our best interests at heart, we have started the work on clearing our life-box for wellness.

Fear of not being good enough keeps us firmly in our life-box behind our prison walls. Even if we think we don't care, when we are unaware we are affected by other's commentary on our work, our ideas, and values. We have a need for external approval to make us feel good about ourselves. Enter the Ego who keeps good company with Fear. Of course, there is a place for Fear, whose job as gatekeeper alerts us to any dangerous situations and keeps watch over our safety. We need to acknowledge this but not allow Fear to hold us back from following our passion and our truth. Ego allows us a sense of self, but here we need to be mindful of our ego for it has an innate tendency to dominate the room too. If left unchecked, the Ego will quickly take over, invade and control our life-box.

If we remain unaware of the external noise we unwittingly allow fear into our life-box. And when we are immersed in fear our hearts close and we can't live honestly. We position our small energy in our life-box and ready ourselves for the perceived attack. We are in defence mode.

Many media and mainstream news reports dwell in the negative; they stem from stories that are governed by the dark forces within our society. We need to be realistic about the times we live in, for there is some pretty grim stuff going on. It is hard to face these dark forces that want to drag us down, we default to fear and the need to protect our life-box. Our automatic response is to build solid walls of brick and mortar. Some powerful entities in our world use fear to drive their goals. Fear presents false evidence as appearing real. Media platforms are used to manipulate and distort reality which keeps societies further in fear. People with great 'power' will go to great lengths to protect their life-box.

But there is another side, stories of amazing work done by beautiful souls who do not shine in the spotlight. Their work is done selflessly behind the scenes, working to uplift communities, caring for the elderly, the sick and the homeless. We don't hear enough of these heartwarming stories from the mainstream newsroom.

I believe that there is much good in this world. Instinctively, I seek for the goodness in others. Of course, there are many times I am exasperated by the behaviour of others and disappointed in my own behaviour and reactions to situations.

Although we should be aware of our environment, it is where we choose to focus our senses that become our overriding view of our world. When we direct our senses toward positive and heartwarming stories — we expand this energy.

When we are awake and aware we open ourselves to possibilities and opportunities. We consciously choose which thought filter to use in our interactions and over our experiences. We are guided by our inner self as we take courageous steps to healing ourselves by taking down the walls of our life-box and expanding our energies. This work has positive outcomes for our evolving human consciousness.

Five

Awareness

"Earthquakes happen so the earth moves into a more comfortable place"

~ Deon Meyer

"Sometimes our lives are completely shaken up, changed and rearranged to relocate us to a place where we are meant to be" ~unknown

Our path to awareness often begins when the universe sends us nudges and bumps in the form of upsets in our lives. When we ignore these signs, the universe shakes our foundations a little harder and if we still ignore these bumps and shakes, the earthquake happens. Our life-box is devastated.

We then have two choices. To become bitter and build a new, stronger life-box with heavy security. Or we can reassess, sit with our pain and grow majestically through that which is painful and create our new life-canvas. Only 'painting' on our canvas that which is beautiful and serves us.

As we grow and learn through our new experiences, we have the opportunity to change the window view of our life-box.

When we are unaware we use our life-box as a fortress to justify our actions and reactions. So when our life-box is threatened we immediately and unconsciously raise the artillery to protect our 'fort'. Artillery is the defence mechanisms we use, our go-to coping weapons. To further protect our fort we build higher walls and close our hearts to our abundant life-force. Outside our life-box everything seems scary and unknown.

When we start to become aware usually after a nudge from the universe, our walls start to crumble and we get a quick glance outside our box. Initially, we pull our heads back into our life-box, into our world that we have created, that of perceived safety. But it is too late, we have seen a hint of the possibilities that exist outside of our box. Although we feel the need to return to our place of 'safety' and hide behind our walls, we cannot. We don't always see it at the time; this is a blessing.

How do we become our true selves? Some of us are not ready. We never expand our life-box; when life throws its challenges, we build higher and stronger walls. We become angry and bitter at the world.

Some of us take this opportunity to reassess our lives, we take down the walls and expand energy — this is the magic. We are taking courageous steps into the unknown. These are steps to a more honest life. It is hard and the road can be a little rocky. It is only when we look back that we are able to see the guidance and blessings like twinkly stars lighting the path on our journey.

This is a step to healing and to our true self.

Society creates norms and standards and we should be fearless and brave to stand in our truth. To be conscious and question the norms; do they sit comfortably, are we following the crowd, do we live honestly, freely and in our truth?

Our moment of awareness is somewhere between the nudge and the earthquake. Life may appear chaotic as the earth settles into a more comfortable place. Awareness heightens our senses and as we move from a place of disconnect and begin to wake-up from our numbness, we can feel a bit disorientated. As we experience any changes it is normal to worry about our future, the unknown — and it can feel a little or a lot scary. As we become aware, you may be wondering whether we are powerless and vulnerable to low negative energies? Are we able to protect ourselves from our environment and maintain a balanced perspective? Yes, it is through our increased awareness that we begin to recognise that we decide when to open or close our hearts. It is a choice.

As we become aware we can use visualisation to create our unique protection. I use a protection of soft glittering gold light that is porous and permeable. I visualise this light surrounding me at the times when I need protection from people or situations.

There are many toxic interactions and traumatic experiences we may encounter in our environment. We can use our protection in these difficult situations, and I use this example to show its usefulness. When someone close to us becomes abusive it may trigger anxiety or helplessness; these emotions can be overwhelming and have a damaging impact on our well-being. Mostly we are unaware as we experience an abusive (mental or emotional) relationship, but we start to feel helpless and confused — as the other person in the relationship has taken our power. When the energy in our life-box becomes too uncomfortable to bear during the relationship, it starts to unravel and we experience our life bumps and shake-ups. Through these nudges from the universe, we have the opportunity to become aware, and when we are aware of the abuse, this is our first step to healing.

When we are able to talk to a friend, a counsellor or find another healing route this begins the process of taking back our power. Through this support, we shift from being immersed in the chaos of our external environment to that of our internal awareness. With awareness, we are better able to acknowledge and recognise the abuse and use our visualisation protection as we encounter any toxic interactions. I acknowledge that anxiety is just one example of an emotion which impacts our human wellness. There are many triggers and reactions we experience from our environment that are overwhelming and make us feel helpless. With our awareness, we start to take charge of our well-being as we acquire coping tools to manage our situations. When we are in our power we make healthier choices for our life-box.

Awareness allows us to explore new thought pathways that are useful and constructive as a reaction to abuse in our environment. As we explore new thought pathways we get a fresh perspective of the abusive situation. For example, new perspective allows us to change our thoughts from "I'm useless and deserve to be shouted at" to "my partner is so fearful and in so much pain, that he or she has lost control". "I am not the one with whom they are angry, I do not deserve to be abused". We are now aware of what is happening and can use our protection visualisation during verbal attacks. Alongside our protection visualisation, we use bubble visualisation to catch the negative commentary and suspend these words in an imaginary bubble outside of ourselves. The power deflates as it is suspended and we have the power to choose our reaction to the abusive behaviour.

We become stronger and in a better position to make decisions for our future. As we take back our power we begin to recognise that the abuse is not a reflection of ourselves but rather the abusive person who is trapped in their own pain

Abuse in any form is unacceptable. And often victims and survivors of abuse are caught up in an abusive cycle for many reasons and for many years. Although life seems hopeless there are always choices; by finding a safe space or a counsellor to hold us as we begin our journey to healing and into wellness, we become survivors of abuse.

When using visualisation be creative and use visualisation that is both personal and helpful for you. There are many examples of creative protections that people can use; such as a garden filled with beautiful flowers, sunlight, beautiful lights, angels or colours. A good thing to remember; as you create your unique protection, be mindful of its permeability as it should allow a passage for blessings and love to come in and go out. Protection made from bricks and mortar cannot serve us, it alienates us and blocks off all life.

Protection that best serves us is permeable to keep out low energies and negativity while letting in opportunities, love, and blessings.

Six

Balancing act

"Maybe the journey isn't so much about becoming anything. Maybe it is about unbecoming everything that is not really you, so you can be who you were meant to be in the first place"~ Anonymous

What we are experiencing at the moment feels important however, it is fleeting and temporary. No matter what is happening at any point in time, the certainty is that the circumstance will change. Everything is temporary.

When we experience bad stuff it hurts deeply and when the good stuff happens we feel light and elated. It is all temporary. It is our energy at a soul level that is real, our core consciousness that is ever evolving and permanent.

A friend asked me to include a chapter on how to cope with life's disappointments. Perhaps a tongue in cheek remark however, it got me thinking about regret and disappointment. Time is linear here on Earth, we live our life forward and understand it backward. Without exception, in some form or other we have all experienced disappointment or have regrets. And there is nothing, well nothing short of a time machine, that we can do to change our past. But we have choices to make about our life right now. We should acknowledge our past experiences as learnings and let them go as we start to heal.

Disappointment and success — do these feelings reflect how we measure our expectations of a successful life? Many measure success in material goods, such as money, cars, houses — and although we enjoy material comforts and financial freedom on our human journey, it's just stuff. It is temporary and becomes insignificant when we leave our humanness.

As we wake up and tap into humanity, we understand the true meaning of a life well spent. When we create our life-box in our truth and find our passion, we become role models and mentors to children and young adults. We start becoming involved in humanity's big picture. In our human journey to our true self, we are able to acknowledge that some valuable learnings are shown to us through regrets and disappointments. This is our soul growth through our human experience and it is permanent and evolving. As we encounter our experiences, we make our decisions based on what we 'know' at the time of that specific decision, in that moment in time.

We grow and evolve through our experiences. Some show themselves as disappointments and regrets and others as joy and beauty. As we grow in wisdom; we make more insightful choices for our life-box. We become aware of the thought-filter we choose over our experiences. Through the choices we make we have the power to enhance our human lives and soul growth. This is a part of our soul's practical experiences in our human person — a school for the soul, the growth toward wisdom and enlightenment.

Worldly knowledge is temporary but it is useful in the now and to live in this time we need to adapt to this world. Education is important during our time here as it is the gateway to our future careers and jobs. It allows us more opportunities to enter the workspace and to choose our careers and to work in the field we would like to be involved. Work gives us access to one of the fundamental energies of this time on planet Earth; money. Our financial well-being and freedom allow us a more comfortable life as it negotiates our access to shelter, food, safety and education.

Education is a conscious learning. We learn in school that which is popular of the time in which we live; whoever is in charge determines the literature we use for our learnings that apply to the history, laws, methods in mathematics and the sciences of the time. It is fluid, and it allows us to mainstream into the now — to become part of the system, to get an education.

Although an education is important for our time here, it is not only what we learn in facts and figures but how we experience the learning environment and how we were taught that will impact us forever. Was love at the root of discipline as a deep commitment to our wholeness as a human being? Or was it a cruel and unloving environment? We need to acknowledge here that we are all affected by our history.

Other questions to consider are, is education building an interactive or competitive world? Are we building human beings as a consciousness whole or attending to the students with their 'hands up' and letting some slip through the cracks'? Do we work in teams, acknowledging individual strengths and that the sum is greater than its parts — or do we encourage individual success?

Soul learning takes place beyond the parameters of the curriculum. It is the philosophy of the education we receive, the lessons we learn along the way such as humility and kindness. Believing in ourselves and acknowledging that success is not a straight line but rather is reflective. The greatest successes are those which touch team humanity.

The window of our life-box is how we perceive our experience as learning or failure. Through the philosophy of finding growth through learnings which show themselves as failures, we understand that mistakes are part of the journey that leads us to become empathetic towards others, rather than judgmental. This is a lesson of the soul.

The world is in a state of constant change and we need to be flexible. Like a healthy plant swaying in the wind enjoying the sunshine, sometimes lashing about in the storm but free from the restraints of the walled-up life-box. If we are not in wellness we will wither, dry up and surely snap in the stormy season of life.

Seven

Relationships

"Despite how open, peaceful, and
loving you attempt to be, people can
only meet you, as deeply as they've
met themselves" ~ Matt Kahn

Often we hear that the traits we see in people that
we don't align ourselves with are the very things
which lie unresolved in ourselves. While this may be
true, do not let this deter you from your intuition.
That vibration deep inside you that warns of potential
harm or sings songs of joy as you encounter a soul
you were destined to meet; trust this process. These
souls were pre-destined to bring lessons, growth,
support, and love.

Sometimes we do not feel safe in our relationships, despite the fact we can't explain why and what is causing that feeling, we should trust our 'gut' feelings. This is our intuition that speaks from our soul, the all-knowing truth. There are people living around us who are in much pain, they are not ready for healing. They have their own path to follow. Be kind, if they are creating a toxic environment — you might need to let them go. Let them go with love.

On forgiving, we need to forgive others for the pain they have caused us. Not because they always deserve our forgiveness but if we do not forgive, they will have our power and we will not be able to move on.

It is important to mention the problem guy in the woodpile, the errant Ego. Ego determines the thought filter we choose to put on an experience. Big Ego is a hindrance in relationships both in our work and personal lives as it can cause us many heartaches and detours along our journey, it allows Fear a loud voice and it wants to be fed. Big Ego wants to be the best, it wants to be right, it wants power and can be motivated by the material world.

Inflated Ego wears full body armour in its perceived safety behind the walls of the life-box and it is on high alert for perceived threats. We all have an ego which allows us a sense of self; however, we need to be aware of inflated Ego as its intent is to keep our energy small and firmly in our life-fort. It ensures that we have our defences ready to wage war to protect our life-box. It seeks approval. There is no place for big Ego if we are to open our hearts and live honestly with real love at our core. It prevents us from loving others, it is hell-bent on being the best and it says, "Look at me, look at me" sometimes crushing others to make the self look good. This is not helpful for the advancement of the collective consciousness.

When we are aware of our ego we are better able to manage our reactions in all our relationships. We become more authentic in our interactions with other humans beings.

As surely as plants need food, water, and sunshine to thrive in our garden, so it is that we should nurture the relationships in our life.

When we walk through our life partially blinded, we don't know what we don't know. We are unable to change if we don't see an issue in our actions. When we are ready and the desire exists, we will open our hearts and minds for us to challenge the status quo. Then we can grow in understanding and love.

Each of our souls have their own unique relationships during our human visit. I include my own path where I have and continue to navigate rocky terrains both emotionally and spiritually. The journey is challenging and it is joyful. And it is a path back to our true self.

We live in a time where many of us have or may experience separation or divorce in our families. It is an emotionally difficult time for everyone. Through the chaos, we need to be cognisant of each other and all the members of the family who are affected by the changes. The breakup is the story of two people who initially embarked on a relationship with the best intentions. They have spent time together and may have children. Suddenly they must face the heartbreaking reality that the relationship has come to an end. As the relationship comes to an end, big Ego creeps in and we become so focused on winning that we forget the other hurting soul. Big Ego is hell-bent on punishing the other, but there are no winners in this situation. Through the chaos, we can forget our children. We love our children; why would we inflict further suffering upon them by attempting to turn them against one or the other parent. Children already are dealing with the trauma of the parents parting ways — the children are not losing their family, they are not separating from their parents — the parents are separating from each other, and children need to know they have parents who have their best interests at heart and hold them with love. When we insult or bad mouth the 'other' parent, unknowingly we hurt that fundamental piece of our children who love their other parent — often causing lasting damage.

With awareness, we can separate in the relationship, hold the space until such time we are ready to forgive the other. However painful, we can make that choice. As a relationship comes to an end, it is emotional and painful. We are allowed to feel the raw emotions and to grieve the end of a relationship. Through the pain, we should try to be aware and mindful of our fellow human soul who is hurting too. I acknowledge how tough it is to make this conscious decision when we are immersed in our own intense emotions. And we are possibly battling with a partner who using every bit of artillery to defend their own life-fort. Ego has taken over and it is chaos. Try to leave the emotional battlefield and deal with the facts. Take back your power, be kind, be respectful. Let them go with love. It will serve you well in the long term.

In some cases, we are lucky enough to work through the challenges to save our relationship, but sometimes we find the relationship on its knees and we are faced with the difficult choice to save our relationship or to save our souls.

As we grow through our relationships and the lessons they bring, we should practice acceptance and tolerance of other human souls on the journey. Remembering that we all have our unique path and it cannot be modified or moulded to fit another person's version of the story. None of us are perfect, we are a work in progress. Some of this work as we move toward our authentic self can be exceptionally hard — be kind always.

Eight

Workspace

Is your work aligned with your passion?

I stepped out of my comfort zone to extend my life-box and changed the direction of my work. My work life started in the travel industry. I was blessed and I am thankful for the opportunities and experiences I gathered along my way. This time in my life was greatly impacted as I encountered unwitting mentors, guiding and teaching souls — some of the brightest and darkest souls showed themselves. I have much gratitude for these encounters and lessons learnt.

My passion for my counselling work is continuously reaffirmed and the souls I am privileged to guide on their journeys are from many different socio-economic backgrounds, cultures and races. This has given me all the proof I need to confirm that we are truly one soul.

There is a reason we should question ourselves about how we are experiencing our work life and if we are passionate about the work we do. In this time of modern medicine and a relatively healthier lifestyle, our life expectancy has increased over the past twenty years and is set to increase even more in the next few decades to follow.

So financially, mentally, physically and spiritually retiring isn't a viable option anymore. If we are approaching forty, fifty, sixty or seventy years of age and if we are not in a job we embrace or loving our work, we can take the opportunity to start a new business or even take a new career path. At this stage in our lives, we have accumulated valuable life and work experience. We may have another fifty years of this life on Earth so how are we going to spend it?

Let us find our passion, align it with our work, take the journey and the rest will follow.

Many of us worry about our financial situation as we are dependent on our salary. To follow our passion does not mean we throw caution to the wind and be reckless. We can, however, start to put plans in place to have our own business, study further or do work that aligns with our passion and slowly make the transition. We should all have a mental picture of how we see our ideal life, then we can work towards achieving this picture. With each decision we take, we should ask ourselves; is this decision taking us toward or away from this picture.

If our intent is clear and we set our focus on doing something we love, it marks the start of the journey — look for the signs and opportunities. Remember it is not a straight line. It is amazing when we start to realise our dreams, we ignite our passion. Align career with passion and it will not feel like work at all, it will feel like Life.

For those of you who are at school or university, the world is constantly changing and some of you will be doing work and have jobs that have not even shown themselves yet. If you are unsure about your future; choose subjects at school you enjoy, pursue courses and university modules that bring joy. Do what you are good at and not what others expect of you. Follow your heart and your passions as we each have our own unique path in this world. Attitude is the most important work tool we require to propel us forward into our future life.

Nine

Experience

"Our mind is looking for an answer
but our heart is looking for a deep,
direct experience with existence" ~
Adyashanti

In this time, there is a wealth of information at our fingertips that we are able to tap into — anywhere, anytime. There is access aplenty to information, opinions, and ideas of others on the internet. We don't need to leave the comfort of our life-box. We are able to use our platform to argue subjects of interest from knowledge gained and some thought-provoking hearsay of another's perceptive. All this, without the emotional attachment of experience.

Modern technology has expanded and shrunk the world over the past years with great speed due to the access to shared resources. This is beneficial for the advancement of humanity. But we need to be cognisant of this huge leap as it slows down our soul advancement through our human experience. We become humans with vast knowledge but lack valuable human interaction and experience.

Look around anytime and it is clear that smart mobile phones provide the larger part of our entertainment, communications, and information than ever before. We don't have to go far to find friends and facts and we can even work from this smart technology which fits in the palm of our hands.

As life becomes easier and more convenient through technology, it's far easier to watch a movie in the comfort of our home on a laptop. We start to miss simple human interactions like calling a friend and making arrangements to meet up to see a movie, go for a walk or to have a coffee together.

Each person in the family is able to watch their favourite series or movie in separate areas of the home on their personal device. Through this advancement of technology there is less and less opportunity to spend time together with our family and friends. Face to face interaction becomes a unique experience, rather than the norm.

As we put effort into our senses and experiencing life; we see and feel the weather, notice our environment, interact with happy people, angry drivers, traffic jams, all offering a range of experience. And of course, most importantly — human interaction.

I observe the teenagers with their 'wisdom' and knowledge they get from the vast outpouring of information on the internet, and when I interact with this generation I am a little in awe of these souls. What I am becoming increasingly aware of too, is their lack in the experiential realm. They have both intellectual and practical answers to life's problems and relationships. But it's a little like a university degree with no work experience.

We need the knowledge, but to really grow in our chosen field and to grow as a person we require the experience.

Our human beings are transitioning into a new world. As we rewind the western world's timeline by 30 years, to a time when parents were the authority and the most important humans in the family. The children in the family were "seen and not heard" and fitted into their parents lives.

As we fast forward the timeline by 30 years to the arrival of the Y and Z generations, we see that these children are confident and have become the frontline humans in the family. The baby boomers and the generation X appear to be the 'fitter-in' generation.

Perhaps the 'fitter-in' generation is the bridge between the old and new world, carrying reminders of the value of experience and bringing grounding knowledge to the Y and Z generations. Who in turn have the instinctive connection as to how technology weaves through our daily lives. Humanity supporting each other as we navigate the transition into the new world.

There is much benefit as we evolve into the new world. Humans are more accepting and have greater tolerance for another's religion, traditions, and values. Many souls have advanced in leaps and bounds. There is far greater transparency and more information available to explore as we form our choices and make decisions for our life-box. We have a platform via social media to make our voices heard, where once was only mainstream media.

Social media as with any new technology has changed our world. As we unpack the pro's and con's of social media — it is apparent that in using this platform we are able create a marketing version of our life-box. Sometimes evoking other humans and especially young adults to ponder their own life-box. When we compare our 'life-boxes' to that of others on social media, they may appear not to measure up. But it is important that we are aware — real life doesn't allow 19 selfies to choose the perfect post. Real life is beautifully authentically messy.

So it is important in this monumental growth of technology, that we take the time to smell the proverbial roses. To ensure we are experiencing life in a way that are able to continuously grow to love and belonging.

What was once life, is now important work to stay in the experiential realm. We have to find a balance between the advancement of technology and experience, otherwise, it is of no benefit to humanity.

We will forget.

Ten

Self-Belief

"Whether you think you can, or you
think you can't — you're right" ~
Tom Ford

Lack of self-belief is a human condition; it holds us
back from our life. Self-belief stems from the
preconceived ideas we form in our minds about
ourselves through the conditioning we receive from
our environment. This is made up of the feedback
from our parents, our teachers, friends and other
influential adults we encounter in our life. The way
we think about ourselves and our abilities is what
we manifest.

Thought plays an important role in self-belief and we should be mindful and conscious in our thinking because thought impacts action. Crippling thoughts such as "I am not good enough" sabotage our opportunities because we are afraid of failure. We hold ourselves back from being comfortable on our human journey — holding us back from travelling our path.

Self-belief plays its part in driving our life-box toward our goals. Many of us will have times in our life when we feel unworthy and have little belief in ourselves and our abilities. Ego plays a lead role here too, as Ego takes over we become more concerned with how others will see us rather than being our authentic self. When the Ego is on the lookout for approval our true self is hidden behind the brick walls of our life-box.

How do we turn this around? How do we become comfortable and authentically ourselves? When we are aware of our ego — we become more aware of our unique coping and defence mechanisms that we use in our interactions with others. With awareness, we have the choice to take down the walls of our life-box. When we put down the masks we wear we are able to bring our true self as we interact with our life experiences and opportunities.

Together with the awareness of our ego and being conscious of our thought filter, we can consciously change our thought pathway. The classic example used to show this is the drive to work. There are many different roads and routes to work but we tend to travel the same route each day and some days we drive on autopilot with absolutely no awareness. This is the same for our thoughts which are unaware and habitually travel along the same thought pathway when in fact there are other pathways we can choose. When we are aware we have the power to make our choice as to which thought pathway to travel.

When our automatic response to a situation is that we are not good enough, not qualified enough or not ready to take this opportunity, is to catch this thought; then change our thought filter.

We do this by remembering a time in our lives when we have felt good about ourselves or have achieved something which made us feel worthy. Remember that feeling and each time we have a negative thought, catch it and replace that thought with our 'feel-good vibe' filter. It takes work and practise, the more we practise the better we get at it. We can choose which filter, negative or positive, to use as we experience opportunities that come our way.

We should never worry about matching up to anyone else or their expectations. Be yourself and remember others are also struggling with their own self-worth.

When we become conscious of our thoughts we are able to question why we feel this way. We often find the answer is fear, fear we will fail, fear we are not good enough, we fear what others will think of us. Enter inflated Ego.

Why do we worry what others think? The people who are our biggest supporters, some of our friends and family will be there to take the journey with us.

Those we are worried about are the 'they' who are not taking an active and ongoing interest in our well-being. They are also human beings who are struggling on their own path. We should be kind to ourselves and support and encourage our fellow humans. It takes work to break old habits, but this work soon becomes the new norm as we change our thought filters and attitude toward ourselves and others.

Lack of self-belief is one of the biggest obstacles that hold us back from living our life to the fullest and deters us from being our authentic self and following our passions.

When we experience disappointment, we can choose to be defeated or to take this opportunity to grow and to learn. To take our learnings and experiences, dust ourselves off, re-pack the knapsack and set off toward a more comfortable and authentic self.

If we have a positive attitude, we are able to learn, grow, and succeed in our work. On the other hand, we can have all the skills required for the job but if we do not arrive armed with a good attitude — it will not be worth very much.

As John Burroughs a literary naturalist; said, "A man can fail many times, but he isn't a failure until he begins to blame somebody else" (1837-1921).

Eleven

Meditation and Prayer

"To make choices that are right for you, you have to get in touch with your soul. To do this, you need to experience solitude, which most people are afraid of because in the silence you hear the truth and know the solutions." ~ Deepak Chopra

Meditation, breathing deeply, silencing the mind — we arc drawn to this peaceful place.

Meditation is the gradual quieting of the mind, a mental technique to go to the source of thought, opening the passage for creativity and inspiration. The word inspiration comes from "in spirit" and meditation allows our spirit to speak to us as we connect with our inner being. Deep breathing and meditation connect with our inner self and all that is. Quietening of our minds has healing benefits and as we shut out the external noise we find peace which restores our body, mind and soul. Meditation is a part of every spiritual tradition and some religions use meditation; such as the Christian Benedictine monks who use a centering prayer. Meditation differs from prayer, as prayer speaks to God, and in meditation, our soul speaks to us. Prayer is a religious connection with God. Although prayer can take place anywhere, we find sacred places of prayer and worship in churches, mosques, and temples.

Our religious beliefs are largely influenced by the family, community and country that we are born into and these beliefs are deeply embedded into the foundations of our life-box.

When we respect the beliefs and choices of other humans, we practise tolerance for humanity, and this has far-reaching healing benefits as we expand our life-boxes into oneness.

History of humankind tells us of the Prophets who have been here on Earth, bringing teachings and guidance to humanity through the different time periods in history. Below is a brief overview of some of the established world religions. There are many other religions not listed here which have the same importance and if any notable details were missed, it was not meant. I am respectful of each religion and its intent.

Hinduism is the oldest known religion and has its origins in the Indus Valley, in the time 2500 BCE. (before the common era). Hinduism has been likened to a softly flowing river, its tolerance is unparalleled, it has no dogmas. Yet it is strong and timeless. It has grown over thousands of years on many levels, in the village, in philosophy and texts. The soul is regarded as eternal and unchangeable. This differentiates it from the mind which is as changeable as the body.

Judaism marks the beginning of the old testament, and it was founded in approximately 2000 BCE. It incorporates the life of Abraham and of Moses. Judaism has no formal doctrine or creed to which one should adhere. The "right doing" has always been more important than the "right belief". It has strong bonds in tradition and family.

Buddhism was founded by Siddartha Gautama who was born in 566 BCE. He was named the "Buddha" which means the awakened one. Buddhism separates itself from other religions as it speaks of the impermanence of the soul.

Christianity began at the birth of Jesus. The exact date has not been established beyond doubt, but it is about 6 CE (common era), and it is believed his birth place was in Bethlehem. He is known to Christians as the Son of God. He was baptised when he was thirty years old after a profound religious experience. His baptism marked the beginning of his public life as a wandering teacher. The teachings and parables of Jesus were recorded much later to become known as the New Testament.

Islam began with the birth of Prophet Muhammad (570-632 CE) in Mecca. He is known to Muslims as the Messenger from Allah. The Quran includes the 25 prophets, such as Ibrahim (Abraham), Musa (Moses), Yahya (John the Baptist) and Isa (Jesus). While the teachings of Islam recognise and esteem these prophets, Muhammad is regarded as the "Seal of Prophets". According to Islam, he is the last and final prophet chosen by God to bring His message to humankind. His message is a universal message for all of humankind. The true message of Islam is steeped in peace.

Human religions have spread to various places on the planet, they follow their own traditions and scriptures, revealed in transcripts such as the Torah, the Bible, Bhagavad Gita, the Quran, and others.

World religions bring relief and peace to many humans on Earth. Sadly, some humans have used religion as a cover for their crimes against humanity, and some fundamental religious groups have used religion to justify some of their vicious acts against humankind. There is much healing to be done.

Religions were not born in a vacuum and their stories and messages are intertwined, so we speak of the religious history of mankind.

Spirituality encompasses the holistic connectedness, oneness, and inclusiveness of the conscious whole. It is mindful of the sensitivity, tolerance, and respect that everyone's belief deserves and has a role to play in any holistic personal journey. I am humbled by the healing benefit of acknowledging the connectedness of people. Spirituality is an experience beyond dogma and ideology and one of universality.

Deep breathing taps into awareness allowing us to be peaceful. Breathing can be likened to the interface between biology and soul consciousness. My Wellness Counselling clients find simplicity, peace, calm, and perspective with a renewed energy through using breathing techniques. When we are calm and awake we connect with our inner self opening our creativity and inspiration, through the language of the soul.

When we are born, we receive our first gift, the gift of breath. In most cases, newborn babies give a hearty cry at birth, open their lungs and take a big breath of life. Readying themselves for the human journey. A child in the growing years hopefully experiences laughter, playing, fun, games — lots of breathing. As we grow into adulthood, life is more challenging and as we take on more responsibility and stress, we unknowingly hold our breath and only breathe when necessary. I have experienced clients who have not breathed properly in a counselling session, except for the odd intake of breath when necessary. You've heard the sayings "I held my breath" and "phew I can breathe again" during and after stressful times. Regardless of what is happening, we need to breathe. Breathing is the foundation for life and healing.

Quiet can be in the form of a mountain walk, a swim or surf in the ocean, or a yoga or pilates class. In the quietening of our minds, we restore body, mind, and soul. We are then able to suspend the external noise that is the chaos in our world.

Twelve

Earth and our world

"When the power of love overcomes
the love of power the world will
know peace" ~ Jimi Hendrix

One of the main stories of our time is power.
Again appears the inflated Ego. The politicking,
religious extremists and powerful entities use fear to
control humankind. If we buy into this fear, these
forces and their puppeteers will continue to rule; and
chaos will prevail. If we stand together and connect
with our inner truth, we become aware of the
distraction that is the external noise of manipulation
and fear. When we are aware we open the passage of
the journey to a harmonious planet.

We see many examples of entities and individuals whose power holds society and communities in fear. For example, during the apartheid years in South Africa, propaganda led to a nation of imbalance, fear and mistrust. Government purposefully kept people segregated — people became fearful and were wary of other humans with a different skin colour. This history has had far-reaching effects and is still in the healing process.

Fear, when we allow it to have an overarching voice is destructive and has the ability to turn people against each other. We need to put fear in its rightful place, align with humanity and know that deeply we are all the same. We need to ask who is behind fear driven chaos, who or what is driving it? To what purpose?

Media advertising is used to provoke inadequacy. Real happiness is not good for some big powerful establishments, if what we needed was enough — why would we want more. Some corporations depend on us feeling that we are missing out. Marketing is driven to make us feel that we will not be happy if we are not wearing the latest clothing, driving a new car, being a certain size or trying out a new perfume.

We live in a time of social media as a platform for uncensored commentary. Information and opinions are free and fast and there is a large dose of ignorance as people speak out about religions and personal lifestyle choices of other human souls.

We need to ask ourselves the all-important question. Why do we fear the choices of other human beings, why does it threaten our life-box? We have much work to do in finding the ability to live our truth and at the same time to find tolerance and acceptance for the truth, value system and choices of others. When we are awake and aware we recognise the part polarity plays in keeping us separate, but we are one — human race. And although we are all connected, each of us is having a unique experience.

We live in exciting times as the world is changing. We are a part of this change and as we evolve toward a conscious whole we can overcome fear and increase the power of love. We can all participate. Our small actions are able to change the face of all things, like a stone thrown into a river, the ripples and effect continue long after the stone has disappeared.

We are here temporarily — the Earth will be here long after we have departed and how we leave Earth is up to us. It is humbling to realise how long the oceans and the mountains have been here before us and they will be here long after we are gone.

We have an opportunity to change humanity on planet Earth and propel our soul evolvement. We have a moment in time to make a difference and leave our mark for the future — to be pioneers in creating a harmonious planet.

If we took a global questionnaire to ask what the world's population would wish for, mostly the answer would be "world peace". And almost everyone agrees "wouldn't that be nice". It seems this is the underlying intention, human souls wanting something different on Earth. We have a choice to stay in fear or to wake-up and stand together and make a new world. To find our collective voice and expand the circle of love.

As we become aware of malevolent low energies, we should neither ignore or focus on these energies. If we don't give fuel to the fire, by focusing or ignoring — the power dwindles as it cannot sustain when there is no energy and oxygen with which to fight.

It's just noise.

Thirteen

Letting go of that which no longer serves us

> "In the end, only three things matter: how much you loved, how gently you lived, and how gracefully you let go of things not meant for you." ~ Buddha

If we are still holding on to people, ideas, and values that no longer serve us — it is time to let go. This energy is draining as it keeps us trapped in repetitive spiral patterns.

It is hard to let go. There comes a season when we know, it is time. It is painful to let go of a person, a place or even a value who has kept us company on our path. If we ignore these signs and nudges, the earthquake occurs and the universe presents upheavals. These opportunities allow us to let go of that which no longer serve us. Letting go requires more than just a thought, it is an active experience of willingness to be free from that which is holding us back from our life. Is it not always an easy process and we grieve our loss — we are angry, sad and confused. With time we can honour what has been before, we are better able to acknowledge our experiences, our stories and the part they play in our humanness. We make peace by letting go of that which has no place in the now. There will be new opportunities that show themselves. As they present themselves we decide to walk into the room or not. We should not stand in the doorway of indecision as it blocks other opportunities from entering our human experience.

Let go of belief systems that no longer serve us. Banish defence mechanisms we use to 'protect' us from the world. Put them down and let them go and embrace the world with an open heart and with love. And with our permeable protection if need be.

As we unite as a community we are able to start the shift in our collective consciousness. We begin this change by letting go of outdated ideas and start to put into place new ideals for our world.

Fourteen

Healing

Guiding with love, free from judgement — allowing inner resources to light the path to transformation.

Healing does not mean that the damage never existed but that the hurt of the past no longer controls us. As we start on our path to wellness and healing we acknowledge that our first step is awareness. This usually begins sometime between the nudge and the earthquake.

Awareness is the powerful switch from the external control to our internal control. When we are aware of the external noise, we can make a conscious decision to get involved with the noise or to suspend it as we connect with our inner self. As we find our way to our internal compass and are not driven by external markers, we connect with our truth and we can feel what is resonating and comfortable in the quiet moments of our being. If we choose to quiet our minds and connect with our inner being, we are inspired as our creativity is accessed and we become the creators of our life-box. We make decisions which will be good for ourselves and for humanity.

Awareness of our existence shows our discomfort in our energy as our life-force is drained because we perpetually live our lives for 'others'. It is hard work to maintain a persona which is not true to our own nature. We are too uncomfortable to carry on living in our life-box that is too small. We become aware of the need to expand our energies to break free from our restrictive life-box.

We start to understand and acknowledge that we cannot control the behaviour of others, we can only control our reactions to their behaviour. We take back our power through forgiveness, forgiving ourselves and others so we can to move on with our lives. If we are still carrying the hurts of the past, they have our power. Although some people do not deserve our forgiveness, we need to forgive them anyway so that we can let them go.

We acknowledge and accept our story as part of our human experience. We should all have a safe space to unpack our story — this can be in writing or telling. Part of our healing is acknowledging that our story is one of our stories, it is not who we are. It does not mean that this story did not take place but that we can find acceptance in the part it played in our human story. It is a chapter in our life book. We make space to start our new story. We are the writers of our future story and we choose the thought filters we use over our experiences. We create, live and explore beyond the life-box. Our previous chapters are learnings and are not allowed to hold us back from living our lives.

Healing allows us to stand in our raw vulnerability and to be courageous as we take stock of our learnings and reassess our lives. Bravely we are letting go of stories, people, and values that no longer serve us.

Find the courage to make changes and to live through the 'aftershocks'. By upsetting the 'apple cart' your world will fall into a more comfortable place, as does the earth after an earthquake.

Healing is holistic, it includes the choices we make on a physical, emotional, mental and spiritual level. Healing embraces the walk toward aligning, balancing and creating harmony whilst interfacing the physical, emotional, the mind and spiritual bodies.

The physical self and the mental self are integral to our humanness and our emotional body is the bridge that connects to our spiritual body.

Wellness Counselling supports and guides our emotional well-being, checking in with our physical, mental and spiritual wellness. It is a safe place for our pain body to acknowledge and integrate traumatic events, stresses over a long period of time or any other difficulties we are experiencing in our lives. It allows us a space to unpack our stories, the ones we have created from our memories — our unique view from our life-box. We start to take down the solid brick walls which are our coping and defence mechanisms. We shift our cognitive pathways and change our thought filters over our experiences as we become unstuck from our restrictive life-box. A safe space that supports our emotional healing through awareness.

We all have a unique life-box and map to healing.

When we are unconsciously surviving we cut off our life force. When this happens, our physical body can present our emotional self through physical ailments and illness.

As we become aware of our holistic wellness, we check-in with; our physical wellness which embraces our human gift of breathing as does good sleep, keeping our body hydrated with water and nourishing it with healthy foods. Finding an exercise regime which suits our individual needs, whether it's a walk in the forest or a gruelling super sports activity — as long as it brings joy. Our bodies and minds will benefit and be thankful.

Mental wellness checks our awareness of our cognitive patterns and thought pathways. In re-assessing our thinking patterns it allow us the opportunity to choose healthier thought filters in our interactions, that are kind and accepting. It helps us to let go of judgmental and destructive thoughts, that do not serve us.

Emotional wellness acknowledges our humanness settling into a more comfortable place. We heal through our human experiences, guided by our consciousness. Our emotional body processes the hard lessons that are revealed in order to shift to awareness.

Spiritual wellness questions whether we have isolated ourselves in our life-box behind a bricked wall? Or have we expanded our life-box and created a more permeable protection to filter negativity and allow the flow of love and blessings? Are we able to sit comfortably as we embrace our inter-connected soul consciousness?

As we let down our defences and are able to look at the part we play in our story, this awareness 'awakens' the connection between our humanness and our soul. Are we taking responsibility for our actions and not blaming others? Are we able to be non-judgmental observers which leads to empathy for our fellow humans? Empathy leads to compassion. Compassion leads to Love. And Love is the language of the soul.

Consciousness can be likened to a healthy 'immune system' of our soul. As we untangle unhealthy worldly forces — abuse, ego, fear and societal pressures, we re-design our life-box in wellness.

This story is spoken from my life-box. I acknowledge the wide scope of experiences and human difficulties in our world. Human experience is on a spectrum of how the world is encountered, is it cruel or loving?

In awareness, there is no judgment or comparison of individual human experience as we each have our own path to healing. We live on an infinite continuum of experience. For example, from the human beings currently experiencing and interacting with life in a cycle of poverty, to those who are momentarily experiencing a life of material wealth.

With the immeasurable love, empathy, compassion, sheer determination and passion of Non-Government Organisations and other human helping groups, there are increased opportunities available for humans to step out of poverty. However, we have to acknowledge that there is still much work to be done here in our world to start to crack the surface of the poverty cycle. And those humans who have come into view of and embraced these opportunities, take first steps towards standing in their power through financial freedom and support.

On the other end of the continuum are those in more privileged circumstances who find their emotional well-being plummeting through living, hardships and devastating life experiences. Some have guilt and deem their feelings unworthy of assistance as they compare their worldly experience with another.

All of our connected specks are having a unique experience and are of equal importance to humanity.

Be mindful of the external noise as it is loud and distracting. It lures our human nature to a variety of numbing tools, it drowns out the voice of our inner self and causes us to disconnect. Our disconnected self is unaware as it immerses in the external chaos.

When we are able to quiet our mind and tune into consciousness, we become aware as we connect with the vibrations of our inner voice. The whisperings of our souls are all knowing, relative and deserving.

Fifteen

Being mindful

Awareness, a beautiful awakening

Life here is inspiring, creative and wondrous when we are open to growth and abundance of our life force.

Life happens, we have little control over the external environment but when we are the director and designer of our life, we can choose to create open and permeable life-boxes with spectacular views.

I have similar struggles as you and I acknowledge the hard work that needs to be done to live beyond our life-box. But when we are awake we have choices of how we will experience and interact with our world.

Through healing, we create a clean canvas for our life-box, which is beyond our story and the confines of bricks and mortar. We choose to put on our life canvas only that which is beautiful and deserving.

When we embrace humanity with compassion and empathy we are opening the doorway to Love, and Love is for healing humanity.

I aspire to live my life fully, in my truth and gently nudge you to do the same.

Thank you to all my early reader for your feedback and for cheering me on during my writing process.

References:

Bhagavad Gita: Lord Krishna on the soul

Blood Safari: Meyer, Deon: South Africa April 2009 'earthquake analogy'

Collection Evolution – founder Joe Martino: what Brexit really shows us Facebook posted – 30 June 2016

Deepak Chopra: on the difference between meditation and prayer. Interview with Oprah Winfrey on Super-soul TV (source internet)

Elizabeth Gilbert – Facebook post. 28 May 2016

Five ways education can save us from ourselves: Professor Jonathan Jansen. Vice-chancellor of the University of the Free State. 16 June 2016. In Opinion. DespatchLive. Facebook

Gary Vaynerchuk video: so you turned 50. Facebook post – 6 June 2016

The Human Search for Meaning: JS Kruger, GJA Lubbe, HC Steyn: Paarl, South Africa November 2005

Kerry Kronenberg - Samadhi Speaks - Facebook post. February 2018

Own your space: Bilchik, N & Milner, L: Johannesburg 2016, South Africa (self-esteem)

Reasons to stay alive: Matt Haig (The World) reference

A School called Earth: Luis Miguel Falcao Johannesburg, 2006, South Africa

Through love into healing: B. Weiss Dr: London, United Kingdom June 1998, United Kingdom